SCHOLASTIC

Learning™ Express

Road to NAPLAN* Success

Fractions and Graphs

This book belongs to

....

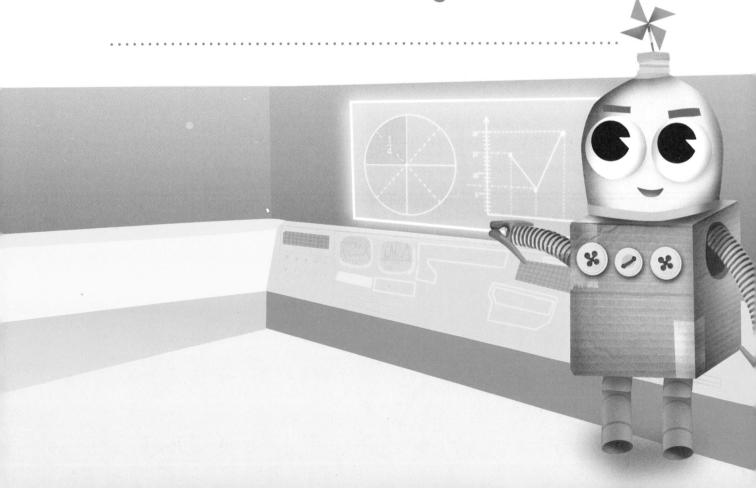

For information regarding permission, write to:
Scholastic Education International (Singapore) Pte Ltd
81 Ubi Avenue 4, #02-28 UB.ONE, Singapore 408830
Email: education@scholastic.com.sg

For sales enquiries write to:
Latin America, Caribbean, Europe (except UK), Middle East and Africa
Scholastic International
557 Broadway, New York, NY 10012, USA
Email: intlschool@scholastic.com

Rest of the World
Scholastic Education International (Singapore) Pte Ltd
81 Ubi Avenue 4, #02-28 UB.ONE, Singapore 408830
Email: education@scholastic.com.sg

Visit our website: www.scholastic.com.sg

This edition 2017

ISBN 978-1-74299-217-4

Helping your child build essential skills is easy!

These teacher-approved activities have been specially developed to make learning both accessible and enjoyable. On each page, you'll find:

Focus skill
The focus of each activity page is clearly indicated.

Meaningful learning
Each activity has been carefully designed to make your child's learning meaningful and fun.

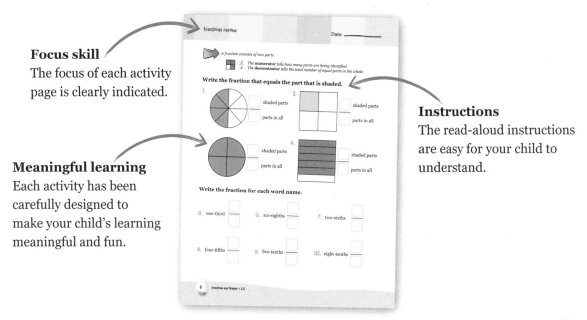

Instructions
The read-aloud instructions are easy for your child to understand.

This book also contains:

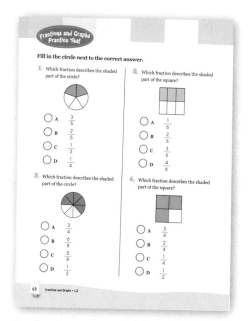

Instant assessment to ensure your child really masters the skills.

Completion certificate to celebrate your child's leap in learning.

Contents

Fractions and Graphs

If your child likes to cook, he or she will find it very helpful to understand fractions. Most recipes have ingredients that are measured in fractions.

Graphs are important to understand because they can show a great deal of information in a way that is fun and easy to read.

What to do

The activities in this section introduce your child to concepts related to fractions and graphing. Read the directions together. Have your child complete the activity. Then together, review his or her work. Reward your child with a sticker for work that is well done!

Keep on going!

Use food to reinforce fractions. For example, have your child count the number of slices of pizza in the pan. Ask questions such as "Dad ate 3 pieces of pizza. What fraction describes the amount of pizza he ate?" $\left(\frac{3}{8}\right)$. Continue asking questions using other family members. Challenge your child to use the information to make a bar graph. Label the vertical axis 1–8. Label the horizontal axis with the names of the family members. Bet you didn't know you could eat maths!

Date: _____

 A fraction consists of two parts.

$\dfrac{3}{4}$ The **numerator** tells how many parts are being identified.
The **denominator** tells the total number of equal parts in the whole.

Write the fraction that equals the part that is shaded.

1.

☐ shaded parts
___
☐ parts in all

2.

☐ shaded parts
___
☐ parts in all

3.

☐ shaded parts
___
☐ parts in all

4.

☐ shaded parts
___
☐ parts in all

Write the fraction for each word name.

5. one-third $\dfrac{☐}{☐}$

6. six-eighths $\dfrac{☐}{☐}$

7. two-sixths $\dfrac{☐}{☐}$

8. four-fifths $\dfrac{☐}{☐}$

9. five-tenths $\dfrac{☐}{☐}$

10. eight-tenths $\dfrac{☐}{☐}$

Date: _____

Fill in the blanks.

Chester Chipmunk was cutting cakes and pies. Bobby Bear said, "Some aren't cut in half. When you cut something in half, there are _____ pieces and both the pieces are of the same _____."

Here is how Chester cut the cakes and pies. Circle the desserts that are cut in half correctly.

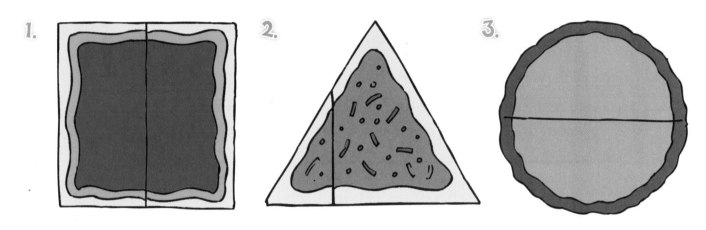

1. 2. 3.

4. 5. 6.

Date: _____

Here is a recipe for preparing peanut butter-oatmeal drops. Gather the ingredients and follow the instructions given.

> **No-Bake Peanut Butter-Oatmeal Drops**
> (makes about 30 3-cm drops)
>
> ⬤ cup peanut butter (smooth or crunchy)
>
> ◑ cup corn syrup
>
> ◔ cup icing sugar
>
> ⊕ cup powdered milk
>
> ⊕ cup uncooked oatmeal
>
> Mix all the ingredients together. Roll into balls. Chill for about one hour. Then eat!

Now study these fraction pictures. Can you write the fraction each picture shows? The first one has been done for you.

1.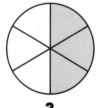

$$\frac{3}{6}$$

2.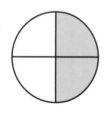

___

3.

___

4.

___

5.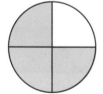

___

6.

___

7.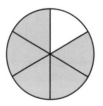

___

8.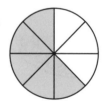

___

Date: _____

 Equivalent fractions *have the same amount.*

  $\dfrac{1}{2} = \dfrac{4}{8}$ $\dfrac{3}{6} = \dfrac{1}{2}$

Write each missing numerator to show equivalent fractions.

1.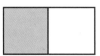

$\dfrac{1}{2} = \dfrac{}{4}$

2.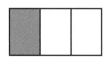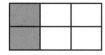

$\dfrac{1}{3} = \dfrac{}{6}$

3.

$\dfrac{1}{4} = \dfrac{}{8}$

4.

$\dfrac{1}{3} = \dfrac{}{9}$

5.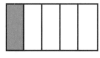

$\dfrac{1}{5} = \dfrac{}{10}$

6.

$\dfrac{1}{2} = \dfrac{}{8}$

7.

$\dfrac{1}{2} = \dfrac{}{16}$

8.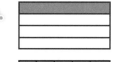

$\dfrac{1}{4} = \dfrac{}{20}$

Write the number sentence that shows each set of equivalent fractions.

9.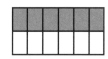

$\dfrac{}{} = \dfrac{}{}$

10.

$\dfrac{}{} = \dfrac{}{}$

11.

$\dfrac{}{} = \dfrac{}{}$

12.

$\dfrac{}{} = \dfrac{}{}$

Date: _____

 Multiply both the numerator and the denominator by the same number to find equivalent fractions.

$$\frac{2 \times 4}{4 \times 4} = \frac{8}{16}$$

Find the missing term to make each pair of fractions equivalent.

1. $\dfrac{3}{4} = \dfrac{15}{\rule{1cm}{0.4pt}}$

2. $\dfrac{4}{6} = \dfrac{12}{\rule{1cm}{0.4pt}}$

3. $\dfrac{5}{8} = \dfrac{\rule{1cm}{0.4pt}}{32}$

4. $\dfrac{4}{9} = \dfrac{16}{\rule{1cm}{0.4pt}}$

5. $\dfrac{3}{5} = \dfrac{\rule{1cm}{0.4pt}}{25}$

6. $\dfrac{3}{11} = \dfrac{9}{\rule{1cm}{0.4pt}}$

7. $\dfrac{8}{9} = \dfrac{\rule{1cm}{0.4pt}}{27}$

8. $\dfrac{3}{7} = \dfrac{\rule{1cm}{0.4pt}}{21}$

9. $\dfrac{4}{5} = \dfrac{16}{\rule{1cm}{0.4pt}}$

10. $\dfrac{2}{3} = \dfrac{\rule{1cm}{0.4pt}}{9}$

11. $\dfrac{7}{10} = \dfrac{14}{\rule{1cm}{0.4pt}}$

12. $\dfrac{5}{6} = \dfrac{\rule{1cm}{0.4pt}}{36}$

Date: _____

Find the missing terms in each row of fractions.

1. $\dfrac{1}{3} = \dfrac{}{6} = \dfrac{}{9} = \dfrac{}{12} = \dfrac{}{15}$

2. $\dfrac{3}{4} = \dfrac{}{8} = \dfrac{}{12} = \dfrac{12}{} = \dfrac{15}{}$

3. $\dfrac{2}{3} = \dfrac{}{6} = \dfrac{6}{} = \dfrac{}{12} = \dfrac{10}{}$

4. $\dfrac{4}{5} = \dfrac{8}{} = \dfrac{}{15} = \dfrac{}{20} = \dfrac{20}{}$

5. $\dfrac{1}{6} = \dfrac{}{12} = \dfrac{3}{} = \dfrac{}{24} = \dfrac{5}{}$

6. $\dfrac{3}{7} = \dfrac{6}{} = \dfrac{9}{} = \dfrac{}{28} = \dfrac{}{35}$

Date: _____

In each fraction wheel, make the fractions equivalent to the fraction in the centre.

1.
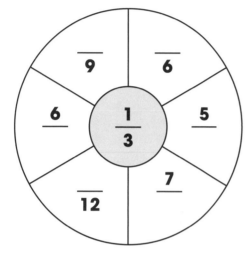

$\dfrac{9}{}$ $\dfrac{6}{}$ $\dfrac{6}{}$ $\dfrac{1}{3}$ $\dfrac{5}{}$ $\dfrac{}{12}$ $\dfrac{7}{}$

2.

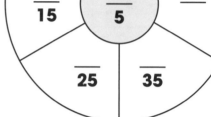

$\dfrac{8}{}$ $\dfrac{12}{}$ $\dfrac{}{15}$ $\dfrac{2}{5}$ $\dfrac{4}{}$ $\dfrac{}{25}$ $\dfrac{}{35}$

3.
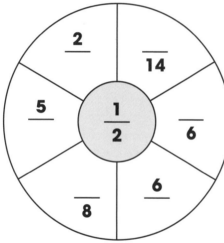

$\dfrac{2}{}$ $\dfrac{}{14}$ $\dfrac{5}{}$ $\dfrac{1}{2}$ $\dfrac{}{6}$ $\dfrac{}{8}$ $\dfrac{6}{}$

4.

$\dfrac{6}{}$ $\dfrac{18}{}$ $\dfrac{}{20}$ $\dfrac{3}{4}$ $\dfrac{9}{}$ $\dfrac{}{16}$ $\dfrac{}{28}$

5.
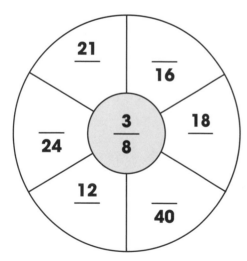

$\dfrac{21}{}$ $\dfrac{}{16}$ $\dfrac{}{24}$ $\dfrac{3}{8}$ $\dfrac{18}{}$ $\dfrac{12}{}$ $\dfrac{}{40}$

6.

$\dfrac{}{35}$ $\dfrac{4}{}$ $\dfrac{}{25}$ $\dfrac{1}{5}$ $\dfrac{6}{}$ $\dfrac{}{15}$ $\dfrac{2}{}$

Date: _____

To reduce a fraction to lowest terms, divide both the numerator and the denominator evenly by the same number.

$\dfrac{4 \div 2}{8 \div 2} = \dfrac{2}{4}$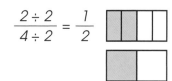

Divide by 2. Can you divide again? Yes!

$\dfrac{2 \div 2}{4 \div 2} = \dfrac{1}{2}$

Divide by 2. Can you divide again? No!

or

$\dfrac{4 \div 4}{8 \div 4} = \dfrac{1}{2}$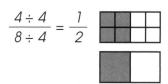

Divide by 4. Can you divide again? No!

$\dfrac{1}{2}$ and $\dfrac{4}{8}$ are equivalent fractions, but $\dfrac{1}{2}$ is in the lowest terms.

Reduce each fraction to lowest terms.

1. $\dfrac{2 \div \boxed{}}{4 \div \boxed{}} = \boxed{}$

2. $\dfrac{6 \div \boxed{}}{9 \div \boxed{}} = \boxed{}$

3. $\dfrac{5 \div \boxed{}}{10 \div \boxed{}} = \boxed{}$

4. $\dfrac{10 \div \boxed{}}{15 \div \boxed{}} = \boxed{}$

5. $\dfrac{4 \div \boxed{}}{8 \div \boxed{}} = \boxed{}$

6. $\dfrac{10 \div \boxed{}}{12 \div \boxed{}} = \boxed{}$

7. $\dfrac{3 \div \boxed{}}{6 \div \boxed{}} = \boxed{}$

8. $\dfrac{3 \div \boxed{}}{9 \div \boxed{}} = \boxed{}$

9. $\dfrac{7 \div \boxed{}}{14 \div \boxed{}} = \boxed{}$

10. $\dfrac{6 \div \boxed{}}{8 \div \boxed{}} = \boxed{}$

11. $\dfrac{5 \div \boxed{}}{15 \div \boxed{}} = \boxed{}$

12. $\dfrac{4 \div \boxed{}}{16 \div \boxed{}} = \boxed{}$

Date: _____

Write the fraction for each shaded box. Reduce to lowest terms. Then draw the reduced fraction in the empty box.

1.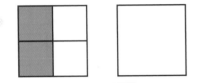

$$\frac{\boxed{} \div \boxed{}}{\boxed{} \div \boxed{}} = \frac{}{}$$

2.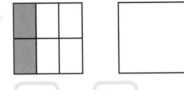

$$\frac{\boxed{} \div \boxed{}}{\boxed{} \div \boxed{}} = \frac{}{}$$

3.

$$\frac{\boxed{} \div \boxed{}}{\boxed{} \div \boxed{}} = \frac{}{}$$

4.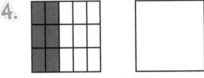

$$\frac{\boxed{} \div \boxed{}}{\boxed{} \div \boxed{}} = \frac{}{}$$

5.

$$\frac{\boxed{} \div \boxed{}}{\boxed{} \div \boxed{}} = \frac{}{}$$

6.

$$\frac{\boxed{} \div \boxed{}}{\boxed{} \div \boxed{}} = \frac{}{}$$

7.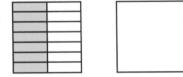

$$\frac{\boxed{} \div \boxed{}}{\boxed{} \div \boxed{}} = \frac{}{}$$

8.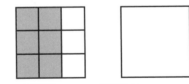

$$\frac{\boxed{} \div \boxed{}}{\boxed{} \div \boxed{}} = \frac{}{}$$

Date: _____

Reduce each fraction to lowest terms. Then use the code to answer the riddle below.

O	S
$\dfrac{2}{4} = \dfrac{1}{\underline{}}$	$\dfrac{4}{14} = \dfrac{2}{\underline{}}$
A	**B**
$\dfrac{10}{15} = \dfrac{2}{\underline{}}$	$\dfrac{2}{32} = \dfrac{1}{\underline{}}$

E	!	T
$\dfrac{2}{16} = \dfrac{1}{\underline{}}$	$\dfrac{2}{12} = \dfrac{1}{\underline{}}$	$\dfrac{22}{24} = \dfrac{\underline{}}{12}$

H	D	N	M
$\dfrac{4}{10} = \dfrac{2}{\underline{}}$	$\dfrac{10}{100} = \dfrac{1}{\underline{}}$	$\dfrac{2}{24} = \dfrac{1}{\underline{}}$	$\dfrac{2}{26} = \dfrac{1}{\underline{}}$
Y	**P**	**R**	**L**
$\dfrac{2}{28} = \dfrac{1}{\underline{}}$	$\dfrac{4}{16} = \dfrac{\underline{}}{4}$	$\dfrac{2}{8} = \dfrac{1}{\underline{}}$	$\dfrac{2}{18} = \dfrac{1}{\underline{}}$

Why was the maths teacher crying?

___ ___   ___ ___ ___   ___ ___ ___
 5 8   5 3 10   11 2 2

___ ___ ___ ___   ___ ___ ___ ___ ___ ___ ___ ___ ___
13 3 12 14   1 4 2 16 9 8 13 7 6

Date: _____

Reduce each fraction to lowest terms.

1. $\dfrac{10}{20} =$ 2. $\dfrac{6}{36} =$ 3. $\dfrac{3}{15} =$

4. $\dfrac{9}{30} =$ 5. $\dfrac{25}{30} =$ 6. $\dfrac{5}{20} =$

7. $\dfrac{2}{8} =$ 8. $\dfrac{6}{18} =$ 9. $\dfrac{16}{24} =$

10. $\dfrac{20}{24} =$ 11. $\dfrac{14}{35} =$ 12. $\dfrac{12}{30} =$

Date: _____

Reduce each fraction to lowest terms.

1. $\dfrac{12}{14} =$

2. $\dfrac{30}{40} =$

3. $\dfrac{8}{32} =$

4. $\dfrac{12}{40} =$

5. $\dfrac{10}{40} =$

6. $\dfrac{15}{30} =$

7. $\dfrac{4}{16} =$

8. $\dfrac{4}{12} =$

9. $\dfrac{15}{21} =$

10. $\dfrac{14}{21} =$

11. $\dfrac{12}{36} =$

12. $\dfrac{21}{24} =$

Date: _____

Use the fraction strips to compare the fractions on pages 19 to 21.

1 Whole											

| $\frac{1}{2}$ | | | | | | $\frac{1}{2}$ | | | | | |

| $\frac{1}{3}$ | | | | $\frac{1}{3}$ | | | | $\frac{1}{3}$ | | | |

| $\frac{1}{4}$ | | | $\frac{1}{4}$ | | | $\frac{1}{4}$ | | | $\frac{1}{4}$ | | |

| $\frac{1}{5}$ | | $\frac{1}{5}$ | | $\frac{1}{5}$ | | $\frac{1}{5}$ | | $\frac{1}{5}$ | | | |

| $\frac{1}{6}$ | | $\frac{1}{6}$ | | $\frac{1}{6}$ | | $\frac{1}{6}$ | | $\frac{1}{6}$ | | $\frac{1}{6}$ | |

$\frac{1}{7}$	$\frac{1}{7}$	$\frac{1}{7}$	$\frac{1}{7}$	$\frac{1}{7}$	$\frac{1}{7}$	$\frac{1}{7}$

$\frac{1}{8}$	$\frac{1}{8}$	$\frac{1}{8}$	$\frac{1}{8}$	$\frac{1}{8}$	$\frac{1}{8}$	$\frac{1}{8}$	$\frac{1}{8}$

$\frac{1}{9}$	$\frac{1}{9}$	$\frac{1}{9}$	$\frac{1}{9}$	$\frac{1}{9}$	$\frac{1}{9}$	$\frac{1}{9}$	$\frac{1}{9}$	$\frac{1}{9}$

$\frac{1}{10}$	$\frac{1}{10}$	$\frac{1}{10}$	$\frac{1}{10}$	$\frac{1}{10}$	$\frac{1}{10}$	$\frac{1}{10}$	$\frac{1}{10}$	$\frac{1}{10}$	$\frac{1}{10}$

$\frac{1}{11}$	$\frac{1}{11}$	$\frac{1}{11}$	$\frac{1}{11}$	$\frac{1}{11}$	$\frac{1}{11}$	$\frac{1}{11}$	$\frac{1}{11}$	$\frac{1}{11}$	$\frac{1}{11}$	$\frac{1}{11}$

$\frac{1}{12}$	$\frac{1}{12}$	$\frac{1}{12}$	$\frac{1}{12}$	$\frac{1}{12}$	$\frac{1}{12}$	$\frac{1}{12}$	$\frac{1}{12}$	$\frac{1}{12}$	$\frac{1}{12}$	$\frac{1}{12}$	$\frac{1}{12}$

Date: _____

Write >, < or = in the box.
> (more than)   < (less than)   = (equal)

1. $\frac{3}{4}$ ☐ $\frac{2}{4}$

2. $\frac{4}{9}$ ☐ $\frac{7}{9}$

3. $\frac{5}{6}$ ☐ $\frac{1}{6}$

4. $\frac{7}{10}$ ☐ $\frac{3}{10}$

5. $\frac{5}{8}$ ☐ $\frac{3}{8}$

6. $\frac{7}{3}$ ☐ $\frac{2}{3}$

7. $\frac{5}{6}$ ☐ $\frac{11}{12}$

8. $\frac{5}{5}$ ☐ $\frac{10}{10}$

9. $\frac{2}{3}$ ☐ $\frac{1}{2}$

10. $\frac{3}{5}$ ☐ $\frac{4}{7}$

11. $\frac{3}{8}$ ☐ $\frac{4}{5}$

12. $\frac{7}{8}$ ☐ $\frac{5}{6}$

Date: _____

Write >, < or = in the box.

1. $\dfrac{1}{2}$ ☐ $\dfrac{11}{12}$ 2. $\dfrac{4}{5}$ ☐ $\dfrac{10}{11}$ 3. $\dfrac{9}{10}$ ☐ $\dfrac{5}{6}$

4. $\dfrac{2}{3}$ ☐ $\dfrac{7}{8}$ 5. $\dfrac{11}{12}$ ☐ $\dfrac{6}{7}$ 6. $\dfrac{8}{9}$ ☐ $\dfrac{3}{4}$

7. $\dfrac{7}{8}$ ☐ $\dfrac{1}{2}$ 8. $\dfrac{9}{10}$ ☐ $\dfrac{10}{11}$ 9. $\dfrac{6}{7}$ ☐ $\dfrac{2}{3}$

10. $\dfrac{4}{10}$ ☐ $\dfrac{3}{8}$ 11. $\dfrac{4}{7}$ ☐ $\dfrac{5}{12}$ 12. $\dfrac{8}{9}$ ☐ $\dfrac{4}{5}$

Date: _____

Write >, < or = in the box.

1. $\dfrac{3}{8}$ ☐ $\dfrac{1}{4}$

2. $\dfrac{4}{5}$ ☐ $\dfrac{3}{5}$

3. $\dfrac{1}{3}$ ☐ $\dfrac{5}{6}$

4. $\dfrac{1}{5}$ ☐ $\dfrac{1}{8}$

5. $\dfrac{2}{4}$ ☐ $\dfrac{1}{2}$

6. $\dfrac{5}{6}$ ☐ $\dfrac{6}{7}$

7. $\dfrac{2}{3}$ ☐ $\dfrac{6}{9}$

8. $\dfrac{2}{5}$ ☐ $\dfrac{4}{7}$

9. $\dfrac{2}{3}$ ☐ $\dfrac{2}{7}$

10. $\dfrac{6}{10}$ ☐ $\dfrac{7}{12}$

11. $\dfrac{3}{9}$ ☐ $\dfrac{1}{3}$

12. $\dfrac{2}{3}$ ☐ $\dfrac{6}{10}$

Date: _____

Add.

1.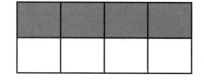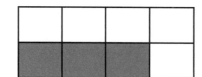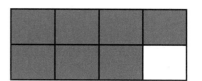

$\dfrac{4}{8}$ + $\dfrac{3}{8}$ = $\dfrac{7}{8}$

2.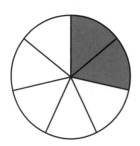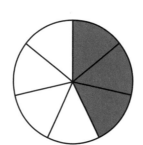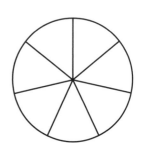

$\dfrac{2}{7}$ + $\dfrac{3}{7}$ =

3.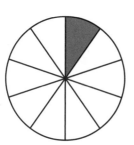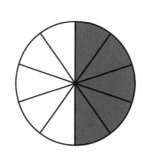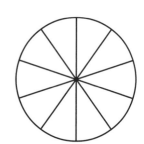

$\dfrac{1}{10}$ + $\dfrac{5}{10}$ =

4.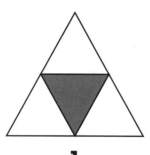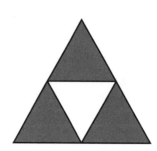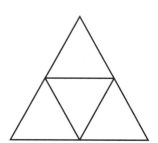

$\dfrac{1}{4}$ + $\dfrac{3}{4}$ =

Date: _____

Add the fractions and reduce to lowest terms.

Example

$$\frac{1}{5} + \frac{4}{5} = \frac{5}{5} = 1$$

1. $\frac{1}{2} + \frac{1}{2} =$

2. $\frac{2}{3} + \frac{1}{3} =$

3. $\frac{3}{10} + \frac{3}{10} =$

4. $\frac{3}{10} + \frac{7}{10} =$

5. $\frac{2}{9} + \frac{1}{9} =$

6. $\frac{2}{9} + \frac{5}{9} =$

7. $\frac{1}{8} + \frac{5}{8} =$

8. $\frac{2}{11} + \frac{5}{11} =$

9. $\frac{2}{7} + \frac{3}{7} =$

Date: _____

Add the fractions and reduce to lowest terms.

1. $\dfrac{3}{10} + \dfrac{3}{10} =$

2. $\dfrac{3}{5} + \dfrac{2}{5} =$

3. $\dfrac{3}{7} + \dfrac{4}{7} =$

4. $\dfrac{1}{5} + \dfrac{3}{5} =$

5. $\dfrac{3}{8} + \dfrac{1}{8} =$

6. $\dfrac{5}{12} + \dfrac{1}{12} =$

7. $\dfrac{4}{9} + \dfrac{2}{9} =$

8. $\dfrac{3}{11} + \dfrac{6}{11} =$

9. $\dfrac{1}{10} + \dfrac{3}{10} =$

Date: _____

**Solve the problems. Then reduce the answers to lowest terms.
Complete the design by colouring the other shapes with colours of your choice.**

$\frac{1}{4}$ or $\frac{2}{5}$ = purple $\frac{1}{2}$, $\frac{1}{3}$ or $\frac{1}{7}$ = blue $\frac{2}{3}$, $\frac{3}{4}$ or $\frac{7}{8}$ = green

$\frac{3}{5}$, $\frac{4}{5}$ or $\frac{5}{7}$ = yellow $\frac{9}{10}$ or $\frac{11}{12}$ = pink

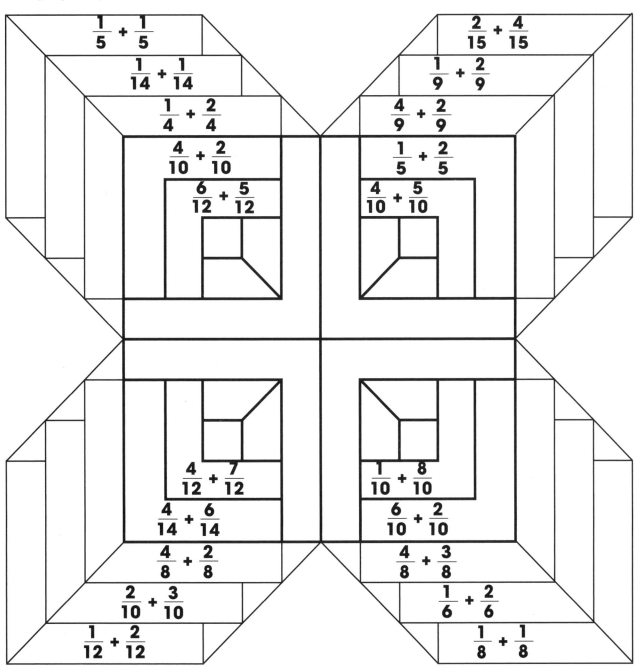

Date: _____

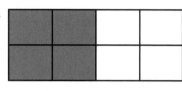
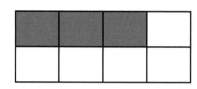

$$\frac{1}{2} \quad + \quad \frac{3}{8} = \frac{7}{8}$$

Step 1: Write equivalent fractions such that both fractions have the same denominator.

$$\frac{1}{2} = \frac{4}{8}$$

Step 2: Add the fractions.

$$\frac{4}{8} + \frac{3}{8} = \frac{7}{8}$$

Add.

1. $\dfrac{2}{5} + \dfrac{3}{10} =$

2. $\dfrac{1}{4} + \dfrac{1}{2} =$

3. $\dfrac{1}{6} + \dfrac{5}{12} =$

4. $\dfrac{3}{8} + \dfrac{1}{2} =$

Date: _____

Add the fractions and reduce to lowest terms.

1. $\dfrac{2}{3} + \dfrac{2}{9} =$

2. $\dfrac{2}{3} + \dfrac{1}{6} =$

3. $\dfrac{4}{14} + \dfrac{4}{7} =$

4. $\dfrac{1}{3} + \dfrac{5}{9} =$

5. $\dfrac{1}{10} + \dfrac{3}{5} =$

6. $\dfrac{1}{12} + \dfrac{5}{6} =$

7. $\dfrac{1}{5} + \dfrac{7}{10} =$

8. $\dfrac{3}{6} + \dfrac{3}{12} =$

Date: _____

In each box there are two fractions that add up to equal another fraction in the box. Draw a box around the two fractions that equal the third fraction. Draw a circle around the fraction that equals the sum of the other two fractions. The first one has been done for you.

1.

| $\dfrac{1}{6}$ | $\dfrac{2}{3}$ |
| $\dfrac{5}{6}$ | $\dfrac{7}{8}$ |

2.

| $\dfrac{3}{4}$ | $\dfrac{7}{8}$ |
| $\dfrac{1}{8}$ | $\dfrac{5}{9}$ |

3.

| $\dfrac{2}{3}$ | $\dfrac{3}{4}$ |
| $\dfrac{1}{2}$ | $\dfrac{1}{6}$ |

4.

| $\dfrac{3}{4}$ | $\dfrac{3}{8}$ |
| $\dfrac{1}{4}$ | $\dfrac{5}{8}$ |

5.

| $\dfrac{3}{10}$ | $\dfrac{1}{5}$ |
| $\dfrac{1}{4}$ | $\dfrac{1}{2}$ |

6.

| $\dfrac{2}{3}$ | $\dfrac{2}{15}$ |
| $\dfrac{8}{15}$ | $\dfrac{2}{5}$ |

7.

| $\dfrac{5}{8}$ | $\dfrac{2}{3}$ |
| $\dfrac{1}{9}$ | $\dfrac{7}{9}$ |

8.

| $\dfrac{3}{8}$ | $\dfrac{5}{8}$ |
| $\dfrac{4}{7}$ | $\dfrac{1}{4}$ |

9.

| $\dfrac{1}{5}$ | $\dfrac{3}{10}$ |
| $\dfrac{1}{2}$ | $\dfrac{7}{10}$ |

10.

| $\dfrac{7}{15}$ | $\dfrac{3}{10}$ |
| $\dfrac{7}{10}$ | $\dfrac{2}{5}$ |

11.

| $\dfrac{3}{14}$ | $\dfrac{1}{2}$ |
| $\dfrac{2}{7}$ | $\dfrac{11}{14}$ |

12.

| $\dfrac{5}{10}$ | $\dfrac{4}{4}$ |
| $\dfrac{2}{5}$ | $\dfrac{3}{5}$ |

Date: _____

Use these chocolate bars to see just how sweet fractions can be! You will need scissors. This is what you need to do:

1. Cut out the chocolate bars along the dashed lines.

2. Work with a partner. Use both chocolate bars to do the activity.

3. Arrange some of the pieces this way to make a whole bar:

			$\frac{1}{12}$
	$\frac{1}{2}$	$\frac{1}{4}$	$\frac{1}{6}$

   Here's how you can show the combination of fractions in an equation:

   $$\frac{1}{2} + \frac{1}{4} + \frac{1}{6} + \frac{1}{12} = 1 \text{ whole chocolate bar}$$

4. Can you find another way to make one whole chocolate bar without using the $\frac{1}{2}$ piece? What would it look like?

5. How would you write it in a fraction equation? _____

6. How many ways can you use the pieces to make whole chocolate bars? (Each whole bar will have 12 pieces.) Draw a picture of each solution on a separate sheet of paper.

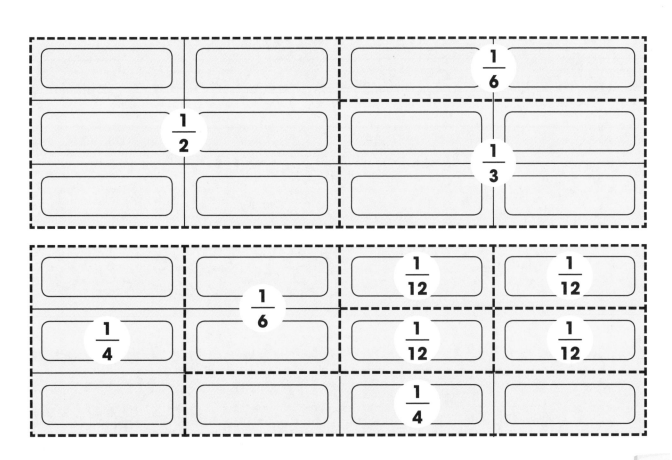

Date: _____

Colour to show the fractions. Then subtract.

1. $\frac{10}{10}$ is the whole circle.

    Colour $\frac{8}{10}$ of the circle.

    How much is not coloured?

2. $\frac{10}{10}$ is the whole rectangle.

    Colour $\frac{4}{10}$ of the rectangle.

    How much is not coloured?

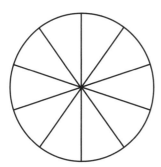

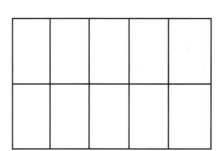

$$\frac{10}{10} - \frac{8}{10} = \underline{}$$

$$\frac{10}{10} - \frac{4}{10} = \underline{}$$

3. Solve this fraction equation. Cross out the dogs to help you.

$$\frac{10}{10} - \frac{3}{10} = \underline{}$$

Date: _____

Subtract. The first one has been done for you.

1.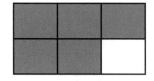

$$\frac{5}{6}$$ - $$\frac{4}{6}$$ = $$\frac{1}{6}$$

2. 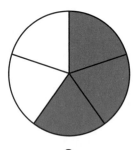   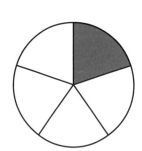 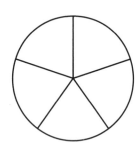

$$\frac{3}{5}$$ - $$\frac{1}{5}$$ =   ___

3.    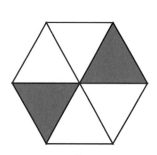 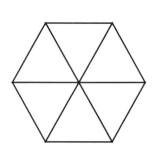

$$\frac{4}{6}$$ - $$\frac{2}{6}$$ =   ___

4. 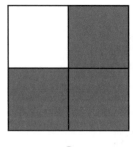   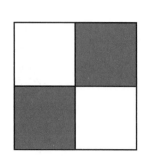 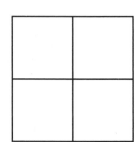

$$\frac{3}{4}$$ - $$\frac{2}{4}$$ =   ___

Date: _____

Subtract the fractions. Then draw lines to match the fraction equations with the correct answer.

   •   •

   •   •

   •   •

   •   •

Date: _____

Subtract the fractions and reduce to lowest terms.

1. $\dfrac{4}{5} - \dfrac{3}{5} =$

2. $\dfrac{6}{10} - \dfrac{2}{10} =$

3. $\dfrac{7}{7} - \dfrac{3}{7} =$

4. $\dfrac{8}{11} - \dfrac{4}{11} =$

5. $\dfrac{9}{4} - \dfrac{6}{4} =$

6. $\dfrac{3}{6} - \dfrac{2}{6} =$

7. $\dfrac{5}{8} - \dfrac{2}{8} =$

8. $\dfrac{4}{7} - \dfrac{1}{7} =$

9. $\dfrac{9}{12} - \dfrac{3}{12} =$

Date: _____

 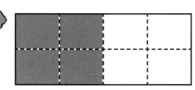   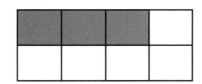

$$\frac{1}{2} \qquad - \qquad \frac{3}{8} = \frac{1}{8}$$

Step 1: Write equivalent fractions such that both fractions have the same denominator.

$$\frac{1}{2} = \frac{4}{8}$$

Step 2: Add the fractions.

$$\frac{4}{8} - \frac{3}{8} = \frac{1}{8}$$

Subtract.

1. $\dfrac{3}{5} - \dfrac{3}{10} =$

2. $\dfrac{3}{4} - \dfrac{5}{12} =$

3. $\dfrac{10}{14} - \dfrac{2}{7} =$

4. $\dfrac{1}{2} - \dfrac{1}{6} =$

Date: _____

Subtract the fractions and reduce to lowest terms.

1. $\dfrac{3}{4} - \dfrac{8}{12} =$

2. $\dfrac{7}{9} - \dfrac{2}{3} =$

3. $\dfrac{8}{9} - \dfrac{1}{3} =$

4. $\dfrac{1}{5} - \dfrac{2}{15} =$

5. $\dfrac{3}{4} - \dfrac{5}{12} =$

6. $\dfrac{11}{15} - \dfrac{2}{3} =$

7. $\dfrac{7}{12} - \dfrac{1}{6} =$

8. $\dfrac{9}{10} - \dfrac{3}{5} =$

Date: _____

Subtract. Do not reduce to lowest terms.

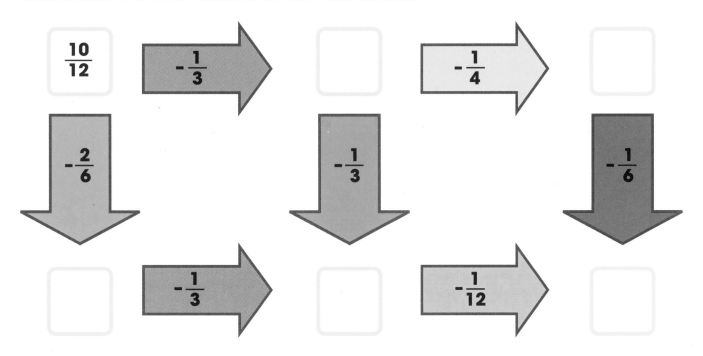

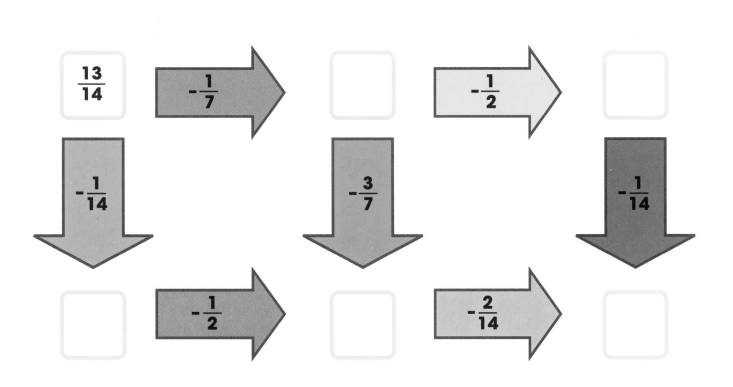

Date: _____

Write the following fractions in the box such that the vertical and horizontal differences between the fractions are the same.

$$\frac{1}{4} \qquad \frac{3}{4} \qquad \frac{4}{8} \qquad \frac{6}{12}$$

Difference

$\frac{3}{4}$	−	$\frac{6}{12}$	$\frac{1}{4}$
−		−	
	−		

Difference

Read the questions. Write the number sentence for each question and solve the problem.

1. May and her sister painted their doll's house together.

    May painted for $\frac{1}{5}$ hour.

    Her sister painted for $\frac{2}{5}$ hour.

    What was the total number of hours they painted?

2. Mother has $\frac{1}{6}$ cup of milk and Joanne has $\frac{3}{6}$ cup of milk.

    How many cups of milk do they have in all?

3. Mike ran $\frac{3}{4}$ km on Saturday.

    He ran $\frac{1}{4}$ km more on Sunday than on Saturday.

    How many kilometres did he run on Sunday?

Read the questions. Write the number sentence for each question and solve the problem.

1. Lisa bought a cake.

   She ate $\frac{3}{7}$ of it.

   What fraction of the cake was left?

2. Joshua ran $\frac{2}{3}$ of the track.

   Benny ran $\frac{1}{3}$ of the track.

   What fraction of the track did Joshua run more than Benny?

3. Belinda filled $\frac{3}{4}$ of a cup with milk.

   She drank some milk from the cup.

   There was $\frac{1}{4}$ cup of milk left.

   What fraction of the cup of milk did Belinda drink?

Read the questions. Write the number sentence for each question and solve the problem.

1. Jamie takes $\frac{2}{5}$ hour to walk to school.

    On Tuesday, Jamie takes $\frac{3}{10}$ hour less to walk to school.

    How long does Jamie take to walk to school on Tuesday?

2. Joe ate $\frac{1}{6}$ of a pizza.

    Jeremy ate $\frac{1}{3}$ of the pizza.

    (a) What fraction of the pizza did Joe and Jeremy eat?

    (b) What fraction of the pizza was left?

Date: _____

Betty and Tracey made some cupcakes. Below are the amounts of ingredients they used.

Betty's recipe

$\frac{1}{4}$ kg	self-raising flour
$\frac{4}{10}$ kg	caster sugar
$\frac{1}{4}$ kg	butter
$\frac{1}{2}$ teaspoon	bicarbonate of soda
$\frac{1}{4}$ teaspoon	salt
$\frac{1}{10}$ litre	milk
4	eggs

Tracey's recipe

$\frac{1}{2}$ kg	self-raising flour
$\frac{1}{2}$ kg	caster sugar
$\frac{1}{2}$ kg	butter
$\frac{1}{15}$ litre	milk
6	eggs

Read the list of ingredients. Then answer the questions.

1. Betty had $\frac{1}{2}$ kg of self-raising flour.

   Did she have enough flour to bake the cupcakes? _____

2. (a) Who used more sugar? _____

   (b) How much more?

3. (a) Who used less butter? _____

   (b) How much less?

Date: _____

Read the questions. Write the number sentence for each question and solve the problem.

1. After a run, Father drank two glasses of water.

   There was $\dfrac{3}{8}$ litres of water in one glass.

   There was $\dfrac{1}{4}$ litres of water in the second glass.

   How much water did Father drink altogether?

2. Jason ran $\dfrac{4}{5}$ km.

   Timothy ran $\dfrac{11}{15}$ km.

   (a) How far did Jason and Timothy run altogether?

   (b) Who ran further? How much further?

Date: _____

The graph below shows the favourite colours of a group of children. Study the graph and answer the questions that follow.

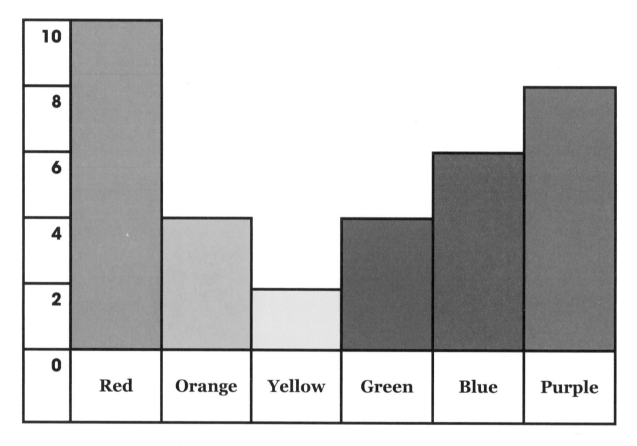

1. Which colour is liked the most? _____

2. Which colour is liked the least? _____

3. (a) Are any colours tied? _____

   (b) Which ones? _____ and _____

Date: _____

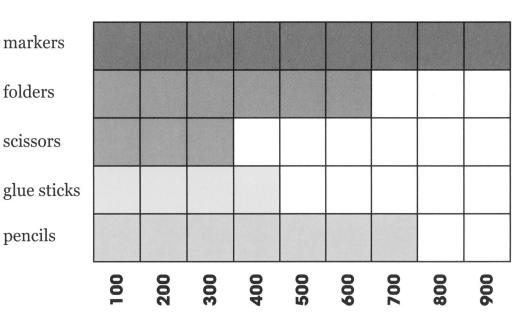

	100	200	300	400	500	600	700	800	900
markers									
folders									
scissors									
glue sticks									
pencils									

Add or subtract. Use the graph to help solve each problem on pages 45 and 46.

1. Mrs Randolph's class used 523 pencils.
   How many are left?

2. Mr Kirk's class used 156 scissors.
   How many are left?

3. Mr Dean's class took 248 folders. Mr Jordan's class took 176 folders.

    (a) How many did they take altogether?

    (b) How many folders are left?

4. Mrs Fenton's class used 96 glue sticks. Mrs McBride's class used 189 glue sticks.

    (a) How many did they use altogether?

    (b) How many glue sticks are left?

5. Mrs Barry's class needs 275 markers. Mr Lopez's class needs 398 markers.

    (a) How many do they need altogether?

    (b) How many markers are left?

Date: _____

The picture was made with 7 different shapes. How many of each shape were used? Colour in the shapes using the code. Then colour in the boxes on the chart, 1 box for each shape used.

10
9
8
7
6
5
4
3
2
1

△ ☆ ◯ ◇ ◯ ▢ ▭

△ = red   ⬡ = green   ◯ = blue

☆ = black   ◇ = orange   ▢ = yellow

▭ = purple

Which shape was used the most? _____

Date: _____

A group of friends listed their favourite fruits as follows.

Name	Favourite fruit
Aloin	Apple
Ben	Pear
Carl	Mango
Danny	Apple
Ethan	Mango
Fiona	Pear
Gill	Pear
Hannah	Apple
Ivy	Apple
Joy	Pear
Kyle	Apple
Lionel	Orange

Fill in the table below with the data collected.

Favourite fruit	Number of children
Apple	
Pear	
Mango	
Orange	

Date: _____

Use the data collected on page 48 and fill in the graph. Colour one box on the graph for each vote.

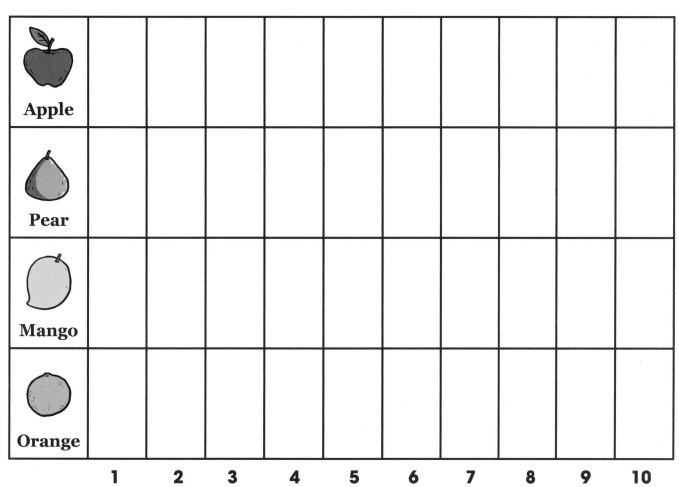

	1	2	3	4	5	6	7	8	9	10
Apple										
Pear										
Mango										
Orange										

1. (a) Which fruit was the most popular? _____

   (b) How many votes did it get? ▢

2. (a) Which fruit was the least popular? _____

   (b) How many votes did it get? ▢

Date: _____

Follow the coordinates to the correct box, then draw in the underlined treasures on this treasure map.

C3 A <u>jewelled crown</u> sparkles.

B1 A <u>ruby necklace</u> can be found.

C5 A <u>golden cup</u> awaits you.

D4 An <u>**X**</u> marks the spot!

A4 A <u>wooden treasure drawer</u> you'll find.

E1 A <u>silvery sword</u> lies here.

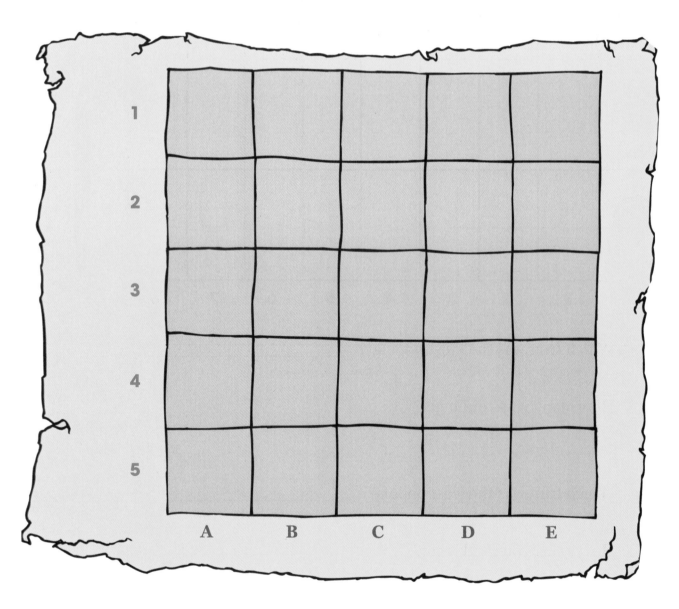

Date: _____

1. Find each number pair on the graph. Make a dot for each.

2. Join the dots in the order that you make them.

3. What picture did you make?

_____

	Across	Up
1.	6	11
2.	5	7
3.	1	7
4.	4	5
5.	3	0
6.	6	3
7.	9	0
8.	8	5
9.	11	7
10.	7	7
11.	6	11

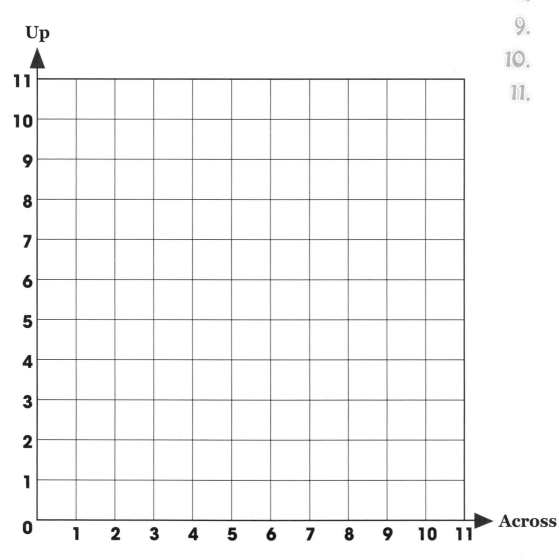

Date: _____

Measure your height and the height of four friends in your class. Record the names and heights in the table below.

	Name	Height (cm)
1.		
2.		
3.		
4.		

Now plot a bar graph with the heights on the vertical axis and the names on the horizontal axis.

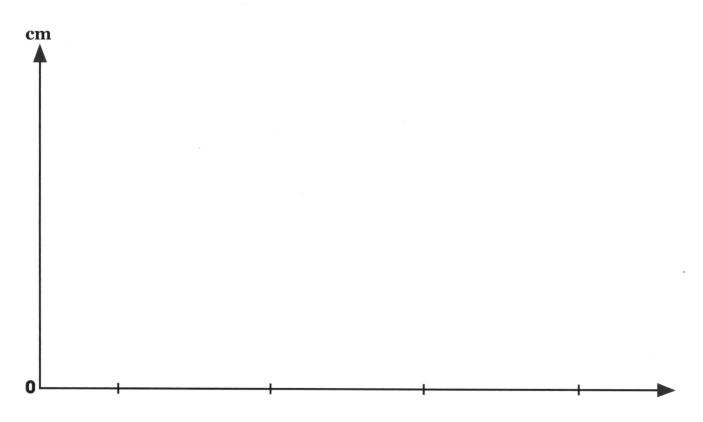

Date: _____

Answer the questions based on the bar graph on page 52.

1. Who is the tallest? _____

2. Who is the shortest? _____

3. What is the difference in height between the tallest student and the shortest student?

4. What is the total height of all the students?

5. Write a question about the graph and have your friend answer it.

   Question: _____

   _____

   _____

   Answer: _____

   _____

   _____

Date: _____

1. Solve each multiplication problem. Example problems have been done for you.
2. In the example problems, the numbers 4 and 8 are called a number pair. We write (4, 8).
3. Look at the graph on page 55. Graph the number pair in the example. Start at 0. Go across to the number 4 and up to the number 8. Plot the point.
4. Plot the point for each number pair, in order. Then use a ruler to join the points in the order you plotted them. After the word STOP, start a new line. Can you solve the riddle?

X → 　　　　　　　　　　　　　Y ↑

Example

| $1 \times 4 = 4$ | $2 \times 4 = 8$ |

1. $11 \times 4 = $ _____　　$2 \times 4 = $ _____
2. $4 \times 11 = $ _____　　$4 \times 10 = $ _____
3. $1 \times 4 = $ _____　　$5 \times 8 = $ _____
4. $4 \times 1 = $ _____　　$4 \times 2 = $ _____
5. $4 \times 2 = $ _____　　$4 \times 3 = $ _____
6. $3 \times 4 = $ _____　　$4 \times 4 = $ _____
7. $4 \times 4 = $ _____　　$4 \times 5 = $ _____
8. $5 \times 4 = $ _____　　$6 \times 4 = $ _____ STOP
9. $4 \times 1 = $ _____　　$9 \times 4 = $ _____
10. $4 \times 6 = $ _____　　$4 \times 5 = $ _____
11. $11 \times 4 = $ _____　　$4 \times 9 = $ _____ STOP
12. $4 \times 7 = $ _____　　$6 \times 4 = $ _____
13. $4 \times 8 = $ _____　　$5 \times 4 = $ _____
14. $9 \times 4 = $ _____　　$4 \times 4 = $ _____
15. $10 \times 4 = $ _____　　$4 \times 3 = $ _____
16. $4 \times 11 = $ _____　　$4 \times 2 = $ _____

Date: _____

Solve the problems on page 54. Then plot the number pairs and join the points. The picture you make will help you solve the riddle below.

I start with an **e** and have only one letter. What am I? _____

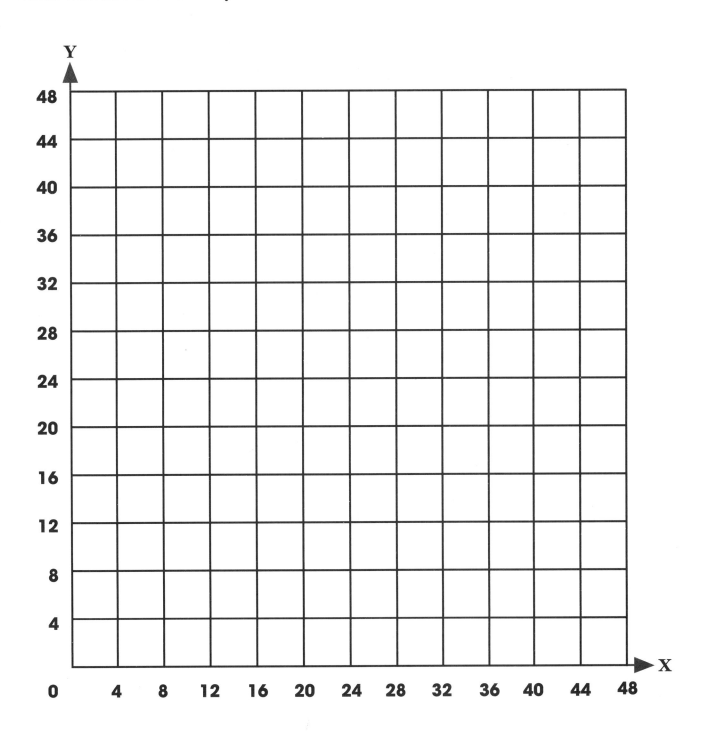

Date: _____

1. Solve each division problem. Example problems have been done for you.
2. In the example problems, the numbers 2 and 3 are called a number pair. We write (2, 3).
3. Look at the graph on page 57. Graph the number pair in the example. Start at 0. Go across to the number 2 and up to the number 3. Plot the point.
4. Plot the point for each number pair, in order. Then use a ruler to join the points in the order you plotted them. After the word STOP, start a new line. Can you solve the riddle?

X ⟶   Y ↑

Example

$18 \div 9 = 2$ $27 \div 9 = 3$

1. $36 \div 9 =$ _____ $9 \div 9 =$ _____
2. $81 \div 9 =$ _____ $5 \div 5 =$ _____ STOP
3. $27 \div 3 =$ _____ $27 \div 9 =$ _____
4. $18 \div 9 =$ _____ $18 \div 6 =$ _____
5. $72 \div 9 =$ _____ $30 \div 10 =$ _____
6. $80 \div 10 =$ _____ $45 \div 9 =$ _____
7. $56 \div 7 =$ _____ $45 \div 5 =$ _____
8. $54 \div 9 =$ _____ $90 \div 10 =$ _____
9. $36 \div 6 =$ _____ $99 \div 9 =$ _____
10. $63 \div 9 =$ _____ $90 \div 9 =$ _____
11. $42 \div 7 =$ _____ $18 \div 2 =$ _____
12. $32 \div 8 =$ _____ $9 \div 1 =$ _____
13. $28 \div 7 =$ _____ $12 \div 4 =$ _____

Solve the problems on page 56. Then plot the number pairs and join the points. The picture you make will help you solve the riddle below.

The older I get, the smaller I become. What am I? _____

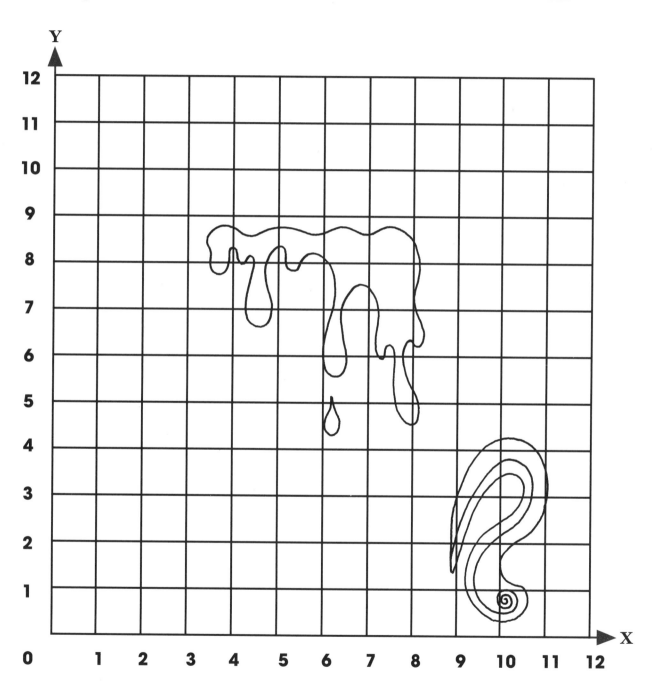

Date: _____

1. Solve each multiplication problem. Example problems have been done for you.
2. In the example problems, the numbers 42 and 14 are called a number pair. We write (42, 14).
3. Look at the graph on page 59. Graph the number pair in the example. Start at 0. Go across to the number 42 and up to the number 14. Plot the point.
4. Plot the point for each number pair, in order. Then use a ruler to join the points in the order you plotted them. After the word STOP, start a new line. Can you solve the riddle?

X ⟶   Y ↑

Example

6 x 7 = 42   2 x 7 = 14

1. **7 x 11 =** _____   **7 x 7 =** _____
2. **7 x 10 =** _____   **7 x 9 =** _____
3. **9 x 7 =** _____   **11 x 7 =** _____
4. **7 x 7 =** _____   **10 x 7 =** _____
5. **5 x 7 =** _____   **7 x 9 =** _____
6. **7 x 6 =** _____   **7 x 2 =** _____ STOP
7. **7 x 2 =** _____   **7 x 1 =** _____
8. **3 x 7 =** _____   **1 x 7 =** _____
9. **7 x 3 =** _____   **3 x 7 =** _____
10. **7 x 4 =** _____   **7 x 3 =** _____
11. **4 x 7 =** _____   **7 x 2 =** _____
12. **3 x 7 =** _____   **2 x 7 =** _____
13. **7 x 2 =** _____   **7 x 2 =** _____
14. **2 x 7 =** _____   **1 x 7 =** _____

Solve the problems on page 58. Then plot the number pairs and join the points. The picture you make will help you solve the riddle below.

I like to fly in the bright blue sky, soaring ever higher — until I meet a wire!

What am I? _____

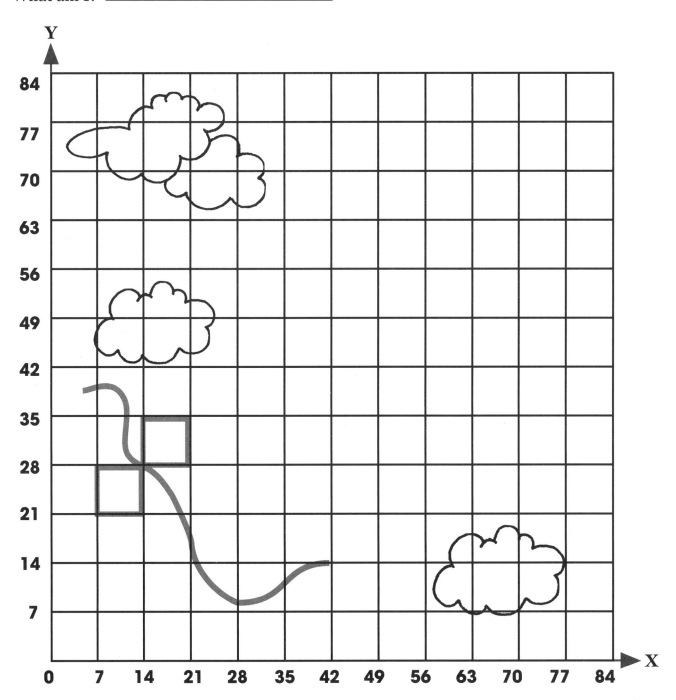

Date: _____

1. Solve each division problem. Example problems have been done for you.
2. In the example problems, the numbers 6 and 1 are called a number pair. We write (6,1).
3. Look at the graph on page 61. Graph the number pair in the example. Start at 0. Go across to the number 6 and up to the number 1. Plot the point.
4. Plot the point for each number pair, in order. Then use a ruler to join the points in the order you plotted them. After the word STOP, start a new line. Can you solve the riddle?

X ➡   Y ⬆

Example

$42 \div 7 = 6$ $7 \div 7 = 1$

1. **77 ÷ 7 = _____**   56 ÷ 7 = _____
2. **70 ÷ 7 = _____**   63 ÷ 7 = _____
3. **14 ÷ 7 = _____**   63 ÷ 7 = _____
4. **7 ÷ 7 = _____**   56 ÷ 7 = _____
5. **42 ÷ 7 = _____**   7 ÷ 7 = _____
6. **63 ÷ 7 = _____**   56 ÷ 7 = _____
7. **56 ÷ 7 = _____**   63 ÷ 7 = _____ STOP
8. **42 ÷ 7 = _____**   7 ÷ 7 = _____
9. **21 ÷ 7 = _____**   56 ÷ 7 = _____
10. **28 ÷ 7 = _____**   63 ÷ 7 = _____ STOP
11. **42 ÷ 7 = _____**   63 ÷ 7 = _____
12. **35 ÷ 7 = _____**   56 ÷ 7 = _____
13. **42 ÷ 7 = _____**   7 ÷ 7 = _____
14. **49 ÷ 7 = _____**   56 ÷ 7 = _____
15. **42 ÷ 7 = _____**   63 ÷ 7 = _____

Date: _____

Solve the problems on page 60. Then plot the number pairs and join the points. The picture you make will help you solve the riddle below.

What did the cricket player buy his wife for her birthday? _____

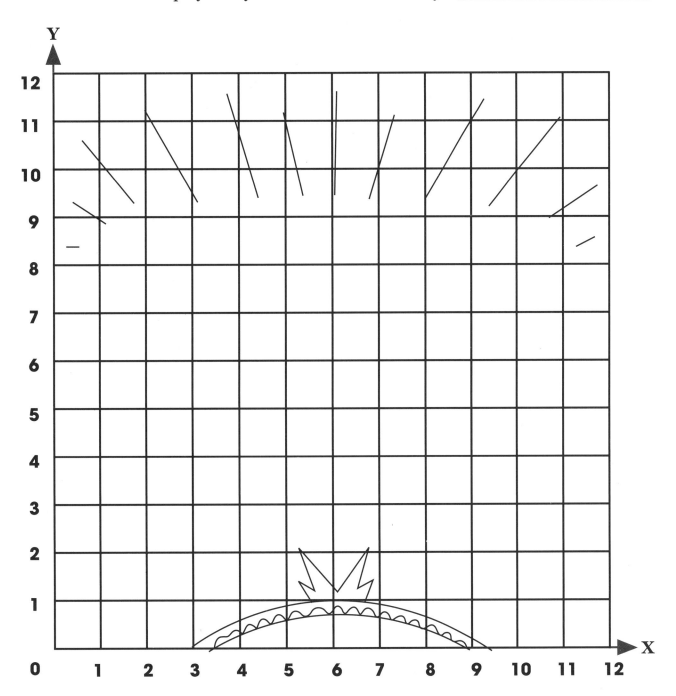

Fill in the circle next to the correct answer.

1. Which fraction describes the shaded part of the circle?

○ **A** $\dfrac{3}{5}$

○ **B** $\dfrac{2}{5}$

○ **C** $\dfrac{1}{3}$

○ **D** $\dfrac{1}{4}$

2. Which fraction describes the shaded part of the circle?

○ **A** $\dfrac{3}{4}$

○ **B** $\dfrac{6}{8}$

○ **C** $\dfrac{5}{8}$

○ **D** $\dfrac{1}{2}$

3. Which fraction describes the shaded part of the square?

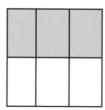

○ **A** $\dfrac{1}{6}$

○ **B** $\dfrac{2}{6}$

○ **C** $\dfrac{3}{6}$

○ **D** $\dfrac{4}{6}$

4. Which fraction describes the shaded part of the square?

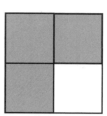

○ **A** $\dfrac{3}{4}$

○ **B** $\dfrac{2}{4}$

○ **C** $\dfrac{1}{4}$

○ **D** $\dfrac{1}{2}$

Add the fractions and reduce the answer to its lowest terms. Fill in the circle next to the correct answer.

5. $\dfrac{3}{15} + \dfrac{2}{15} =$

   ○ A $\dfrac{1}{3}$

   ○ B $\dfrac{1}{4}$

   ○ C $\dfrac{1}{5}$

   ○ D $\dfrac{1}{6}$

7. $\dfrac{2}{16} + \dfrac{2}{16} =$

   ○ A $\dfrac{1}{2}$

   ○ B $\dfrac{1}{3}$

   ○ C $\dfrac{1}{4}$

   ○ D $\dfrac{4}{16}$

6. $\dfrac{1}{5} + \dfrac{2}{5} =$

   ○ A $\dfrac{1}{2}$

   ○ B $\dfrac{1}{3}$

   ○ C $\dfrac{6}{10}$

   ○ D $\dfrac{3}{5}$

8. $\dfrac{4}{8} + \dfrac{2}{8} =$

   ○ A $\dfrac{6}{8}$

   ○ B $\dfrac{1}{4}$

   ○ C $\dfrac{3}{4}$

   ○ D $\dfrac{2}{3}$

Fill in the circle next to the correct answer.

9. $\dfrac{8}{9} - \dfrac{2}{9} =$

    ○ A $\dfrac{10}{9}$

    ○ B $\dfrac{2}{3}$

    ○ C $\dfrac{7}{9}$

    ○ D $\dfrac{1}{3}$

11. $\dfrac{5}{6} - \dfrac{1}{6} =$

    ○ A $\dfrac{2}{3}$

    ○ B $\dfrac{4}{3}$

    ○ C   1

    ○ D $\dfrac{1}{3}$

10. $\dfrac{3}{5} - \dfrac{1}{5} =$

    ○ A $\dfrac{1}{5}$

    ○ B $\dfrac{2}{5}$

    ○ C $\dfrac{3}{5}$

    ○ D $\dfrac{4}{5}$

12. $\dfrac{7}{8} - \dfrac{5}{8} =$

    ○ A $\dfrac{1}{2}$

    ○ B $\dfrac{1}{3}$

    ○ C $\dfrac{1}{4}$

    ○ D $\dfrac{1}{8}$

Fill in the circle next to the correct answer.

13. $\dfrac{1}{4} + \dfrac{5}{8} =$

◯ **A** $\dfrac{6}{8}$

◯ **B** $\dfrac{1}{2}$

◯ **C** $\dfrac{7}{8}$

◯ **D** $\dfrac{8}{8}$

15. $\dfrac{5}{6} - \dfrac{5}{12} =$

◯ **A** 0

◯ **B** $\dfrac{5}{12}$

◯ **C** $\dfrac{5}{6}$

◯ **D** $\dfrac{6}{6}$

14. $\dfrac{5}{12} + \dfrac{1}{3} =$

◯ **A** $\dfrac{4}{9}$

◯ **B** $\dfrac{6}{9}$

◯ **C** $\dfrac{3}{4}$

◯ **D** $\dfrac{1}{12}$

16. $\dfrac{4}{5} - \dfrac{11}{15} =$

◯ **A** $\dfrac{1}{15}$

◯ **B** $\dfrac{7}{15}$

◯ **C** $\dfrac{1}{5}$

◯ **D** $\dfrac{15}{15}$

Fill in the circle next to the correct answer.

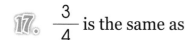

17. $\dfrac{3}{4}$ is the same as

○ **A** $\dfrac{6}{8}$

○ **B** $\dfrac{1}{2}$

○ **C** $\dfrac{6}{4}$

○ **D** $\dfrac{6}{12}$

19. $\dfrac{5}{6}$ is the same as

○ **A** $\dfrac{10}{15}$

○ **B** $\dfrac{12}{18}$

○ **C** $\dfrac{15}{18}$

○ **D** $\dfrac{15}{20}$

18. $\dfrac{2}{3}$ is the same as

○ **A** $\dfrac{4}{8}$

○ **B** $\dfrac{6}{9}$

○ **C** $\dfrac{8}{15}$

○ **D** $\dfrac{6}{8}$

20. $\dfrac{1}{2}$ is the same as

○ **A** $\dfrac{2}{6}$

○ **B** $\dfrac{3}{8}$

○ **C** $\dfrac{5}{10}$

○ **D** $\dfrac{6}{15}$

Fill in the circle next to the correct answer.

21. $\frac{8}{20}$ reduced to lowest terms is

   ◯ A $\frac{2}{2}$

   ◯ B $\frac{4}{10}$

   ◯ C $\frac{2}{4}$

   ◯ D $\frac{2}{5}$

23. $\frac{9}{24}$ reduced to lowest terms is

   ◯ A $\frac{1}{3}$

   ◯ B $\frac{3}{8}$

   ◯ C $\frac{4}{12}$

   ◯ D $\frac{2}{6}$

22. $\frac{12}{15}$ reduced to lowest terms is

   ◯ A $\frac{4}{5}$

   ◯ B $\frac{3}{5}$

   ◯ C $\frac{2}{3}$

   ◯ D $\frac{1}{3}$

24. $\frac{12}{20}$ reduced to lowest terms is

   ◯ A $\frac{6}{10}$

   ◯ B $\frac{4}{7}$

   ◯ C $\frac{2}{4}$

   ◯ D $\frac{3}{5}$

Fill in the circle next to the correct answer.

25. $\frac{4}{7} >$

○ A $\quad \frac{4}{5}$

○ B $\quad \frac{1}{14}$

○ C $\quad \frac{6}{7}$

○ D $\quad \frac{8}{14}$

27. $\frac{2}{9} <$

○ A $\quad \frac{4}{18}$

○ B $\quad \frac{2}{18}$

○ C $\quad \frac{1}{9}$

○ D $\quad \frac{1}{3}$

26. $\frac{1}{2} < \quad < \frac{3}{4}$

○ A $\quad \frac{2}{3}$

○ B $\quad \frac{1}{3}$

○ C $\quad \frac{1}{4}$

○ D $\quad \frac{2}{4}$

28. $\frac{2}{3} < \quad < \frac{11}{12}$

○ A $\quad \frac{3}{4}$

○ B $\quad \frac{1}{6}$

○ C $\quad \frac{5}{12}$

○ D $\quad \frac{2}{9}$

Read the questions. Write the number sentence for each question and solve the problem.

 Mother bought a cake.

She ate $\frac{1}{4}$ of it.

Sandra ate $\frac{1}{8}$ of it.

(a) Who ate more? How much more?

(b) What fraction of the cake did Sandra and Mother eat altogether?

(c) What fraction of the cake was left?

Fractions and Graphs
Practice Test

Read the questions. Write the number sentence for each question and solve the problem.

30. A pylon is painted in four different colours.

$\frac{1}{2}$ of the pylon is painted green.

$\frac{1}{4}$ of the pylon is painted blue.

$\frac{1}{8}$ of the pylon is painted yellow.

The remainder of the pylon is painted pink.

(a) What fraction of the pylon is painted green and blue?

(b) What fraction of the pylon is NOT painted pink?

(c) What fraction of the pylon is painted pink?

Mrs Jean's class took a survey to find out which foods the class liked best. Use the information on the bar graph to answer the questions. Fill in the circle next to the correct answer.

pizza	
sandwiches	
salads	
noodles	
pies	

31. Which was the class' favourite food?

◯ **A**   pies   ◯ **B**   pizza

◯ **C**   salad   ◯ **D**   noodles

32. Which food was the class' second favourite?

◯ **A**   pies   ◯ **B**   noodles

◯ **C**   pizza   ◯ **D**   salads

33. Which food was the class' least favourite?

◯ **A**   pizza   ◯ **B**   pies

◯ **C**   sandwiches   ◯ **D**   noodles

The graph below is incomplete. It shows the pets kept by the students in a class.

34. Read the sentences below. Then draw bars to complete the graph.

2 more students kept pet rabbits than pet birds.

6 fewer students kept pet cats than pet fish.

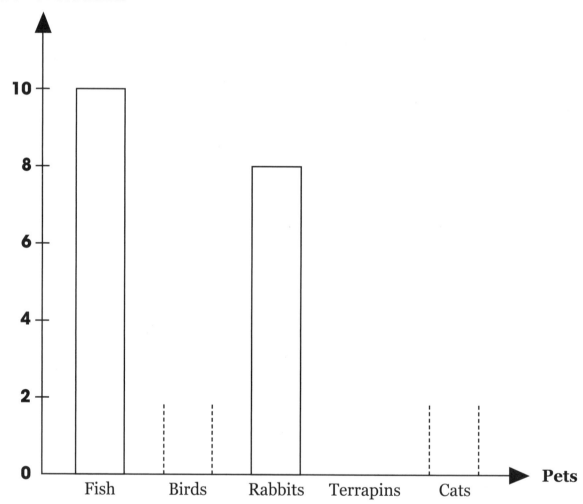

Look at the completed graph on page 72. Fill in the circle next to the correct answer.

35. How many students kept fish as pets?

   ○ **A**   4   ○ **B**   6

   ○ **C**   8   ○ **D**   10

36. How many more students have pet rabbits than pet terrapins?

   ○ **A**   0   ○ **B**   4

   ○ **C**   6   ○ **D**   8

37. How many more students kept pet birds than pet cats?

   ○ **A**   8   ○ **B**   2

   ○ **C**   4   ○ **D**   1

38. How many students are there in the class?

   ○ **A**   18   ○ **B**   20

   ○ **C**   26   ○ **D**   28

39. Find each number pair on the graph. Make a dot for each. Join the dots in the order that you make them. What picture did you make? _____

	Across	Up
1.	9	2
2.	7	4
3.	8	4
4.	6	6
5.	7	6
6.	5	8
7.	3	6
8.	4	6
9.	2	4
10.	3	4
11.	1	2

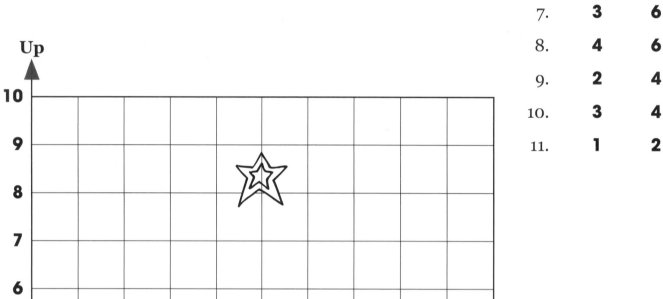

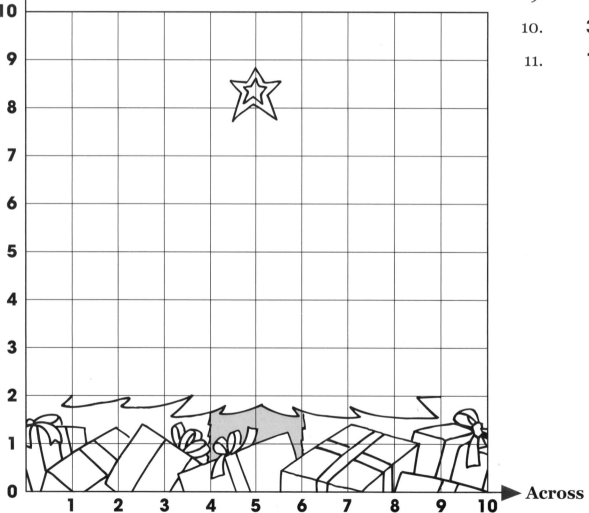

Answer Key

Page 6

1. $\frac{4}{8}$ 2. $\frac{1}{4}$ 3. $\frac{4}{4}$ 4. $\frac{5}{6}$ 5. $\frac{1}{3}$

6. $\frac{6}{8}$ 7. $\frac{2}{6}$ 8. $\frac{4}{5}$ 9. $\frac{5}{10}$ 10. $\frac{8}{10}$

Page 7

2, size; Circle: 1, 3, 5

Page 8

2. $\frac{2}{4}$ 3. $\frac{3}{8}$ 4. $\frac{2}{3}$ 5. $\frac{3}{4}$

6. $\frac{4}{5}$ 7. $\frac{5}{6}$ 8. $\frac{5}{8}$

Page 9

1. 2   2. 2   3. 2   4. 3

5. 2   6. 4   7. 8   8. 5

9. $\frac{1}{2} = \frac{6}{12}$ 10. $\frac{1}{3} = \frac{2}{6}$

11. $\frac{1}{6} = \frac{3}{18}$ 12. $\frac{1}{2} = \frac{3}{6}$

Page 10

1. 20   2. 18   3. 20   4. 36

5. 15   6. 33   7. 24   8. 9

9. 20   10. 6   11. 20   12. 30

Page 11

1. 2, 3, 4, 5   2. 6, 9, 16, 20

3. 4, 9, 8, 15   4. 10, 12, 16, 25

5. 2, 18, 4, 30   6. 14, 21, 12, 15

Page 12

1. $\frac{3}{9}, \frac{2}{6}, \frac{5}{15}, \frac{7}{21}, \frac{4}{12}, \frac{6}{18}$

2. $\frac{8}{20}, \frac{12}{30}, \frac{4}{10}, \frac{14}{35}, \frac{10}{25}, \frac{6}{15}$

3. $\frac{2}{4}, \frac{7}{14}, \frac{3}{6}, \frac{6}{12}, \frac{4}{8}, \frac{5}{10}$

4. $\frac{6}{8}, \frac{18}{24}, \frac{9}{12}, \frac{21}{28}, \frac{12}{16}, \frac{15}{20}$

5. $\frac{21}{56}, \frac{6}{16}, \frac{18}{48}, \frac{15}{40}, \frac{12}{32}, \frac{9}{24}$

6. $\frac{7}{35}, \frac{4}{20}, \frac{6}{30}, \frac{2}{10}, \frac{3}{15}, \frac{5}{25}$

Page 13

1. 2, $\frac{1}{2}$ 2. 3, $\frac{2}{3}$ 3. 5, $\frac{1}{2}$ 4. 5, $\frac{2}{3}$

5. 4, $\frac{1}{2}$ 6. 2, $\frac{5}{6}$ 7. 3, $\frac{1}{2}$ 8. 3, $\frac{1}{3}$

9. 7, $\frac{1}{2}$ 10. 2, $\frac{3}{4}$ 11. 5, $\frac{1}{3}$ 12. 4, $\frac{1}{4}$

Page 14

1. $\frac{2}{4} \div \frac{2}{2} = \frac{1}{2}$ 2. $\frac{2}{6} \div \frac{2}{2} = \frac{1}{3}$

3. $\frac{3}{12} \div \frac{3}{3} = \frac{1}{4}$ 4. $\frac{6}{15} \div \frac{3}{3} = \frac{2}{5}$

5. $\frac{8}{10} \div \frac{2}{2} = \frac{4}{5}$ 6. $\frac{5}{10} \div \frac{5}{5} = \frac{1}{2}$

7. $\frac{7}{14} \div \frac{7}{7} = \frac{1}{2}$ 8. $\frac{6}{9} \div \frac{3}{3} = \frac{2}{3}$

Page 15

O. 2   S. 7   A. 3   B. 16
E. 8   !. 6   T. 11   H. 5
D. 10   N. 12   M. 13   Y. 14
P. 1   R. 4   L. 9;

HE HAD TOO MANY PROBLEMS!

Page 16

1. $\frac{1}{2}$ 2. $\frac{1}{6}$ 3. $\frac{1}{5}$ 4. $\frac{3}{10}$

5. $\frac{5}{6}$ 6. $\frac{1}{4}$ 7. $\frac{1}{4}$ 8. $\frac{1}{3}$

9. $\frac{2}{3}$ 10. $\frac{5}{6}$ 11. $\frac{2}{5}$ 12. $\frac{2}{5}$

Page 17

1. $\frac{6}{7}$ 2. $\frac{3}{4}$ 3. $\frac{1}{4}$ 4. $\frac{3}{10}$

5. $\frac{1}{4}$ 6. $\frac{1}{2}$ 7. $\frac{1}{4}$ 8. $\frac{1}{3}$

9. $\frac{5}{7}$ 10. $\frac{2}{3}$ 11. $\frac{1}{3}$ 12. $\frac{7}{8}$

Pages 18–19

1. >   2. <   3. >   4. >
5. >   6. >   7. <   8. =
9. >   10. >   11. <   12. >

Page 20

1. <   2. <   3. >   4. <
5. >   6. >   7. >   8. <
9. >   10. >   11. >   12. >

Page 21

1. >   2. >   3. <   4. >
5. =   6. <   7. =   8. <
9. >   10. >   11. =   12. >

Page 22

2.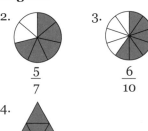

$\frac{5}{7}$

3.

$\frac{6}{10}$

4.

$\frac{4}{4}$ or 1

Page 23

1. 1   2. 1   3. $\frac{3}{5}$ 4. 1   5. $\frac{1}{3}$

6. $\frac{7}{9}$ 7. $\frac{3}{4}$ 8. $\frac{7}{11}$ 9. $\frac{5}{7}$

Page 24

1. $\frac{3}{5}$ 2. 1   3. 1   4. $\frac{4}{5}$ 5. $\frac{1}{2}$

6. $\frac{1}{2}$ 7. $\frac{2}{3}$ 8. $\frac{9}{11}$ 9. $\frac{2}{5}$

Page 25

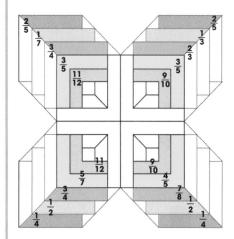

Page 26

1. $\frac{7}{10}$ 2. $\frac{3}{4}$ 3. $\frac{7}{12}$ 4. $\frac{7}{8}$

Page 27

1. $\dfrac{8}{9}$ 2. $\dfrac{5}{6}$ 3. $\dfrac{6}{7}$ 4. $\dfrac{8}{9}$

5. $\dfrac{7}{10}$ 6. $\dfrac{11}{12}$ 7. $\dfrac{9}{10}$ 8. $\dfrac{3}{4}$

Page 28

2.   3.

4.   5.

6.   7.

8.   9.

10.   11.

12.

Page 29

Answers will vary.

Page 31

1. $\dfrac{2}{10}$ 2. $\dfrac{6}{10}$ 3. $\dfrac{7}{10}$

Page 32

2.

$\dfrac{2}{5}$

3.

$\dfrac{2}{6}$ or $\dfrac{1}{3}$

4.

$\dfrac{1}{4}$

Page 33

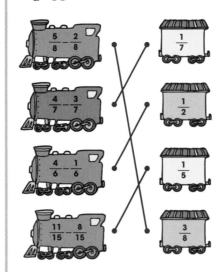

Page 34

1. $\dfrac{1}{5}$ 2. $\dfrac{2}{5}$ 3. $\dfrac{4}{7}$ 4. $\dfrac{4}{11}$ 5. $\dfrac{3}{4}$

6. $\dfrac{1}{6}$ 7. $\dfrac{3}{8}$ 8. $\dfrac{3}{7}$ 9. $\dfrac{1}{2}$

Page 35

1. $\dfrac{3}{10}$ 2. $\dfrac{4}{12}$ or $\dfrac{1}{3}$

3. $\dfrac{6}{14}$ or $\dfrac{3}{7}$ 4. $\dfrac{2}{6}$ or $\dfrac{1}{3}$

Page 36

1. $\dfrac{1}{12}$ 2. $\dfrac{1}{9}$ 3. $\dfrac{5}{9}$ 4. $\dfrac{1}{15}$

5. $\dfrac{1}{3}$ 6. $\dfrac{1}{15}$ 7. $\dfrac{5}{12}$ 8. $\dfrac{3}{10}$

Page 37

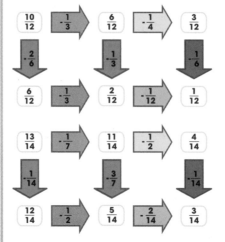

Page 38

$\dfrac{3}{4}$	-	$\dfrac{6}{12}$	$\dfrac{1}{4}$
-		-	
$\dfrac{4}{8}$	-	$\dfrac{1}{4}$	$\dfrac{1}{4}$
$\dfrac{1}{4}$		$\dfrac{1}{4}$	

Page 39

1. $\dfrac{1}{5} + \dfrac{2}{5} = \dfrac{3}{5}$ hours

2. $\dfrac{1}{6} + \dfrac{3}{6} = \dfrac{4}{6} = \dfrac{2}{3}$ cup

3. $\dfrac{3}{4} + \dfrac{1}{4} = 1$ km

Page 40

1. $\dfrac{7}{7} - \dfrac{3}{7} = \dfrac{4}{7}$

2. $\dfrac{2}{3} - \dfrac{1}{3} = \dfrac{1}{3}$

3. $\dfrac{3}{4} - \dfrac{1}{4} = \dfrac{2}{4} = \dfrac{1}{2}$

Page 41

1. $\dfrac{2}{5} - \dfrac{3}{10} = \dfrac{4}{10} - \dfrac{3}{10} = \dfrac{1}{10}$ hour

2. (a) $\dfrac{1}{6} + \dfrac{1}{3} = \dfrac{1}{6} + \dfrac{2}{6} = \dfrac{3}{6} = \dfrac{1}{2}$

   (b) $1 - \dfrac{1}{2} = \dfrac{2}{2} - \dfrac{1}{2} = \dfrac{1}{2}$

Page 42

1. Yes

2. (a) Tracey

   (b) $\dfrac{1}{2} - \dfrac{4}{10} = \dfrac{5}{10} - \dfrac{4}{10} = \dfrac{1}{10}$ kg

3. (a) Betty

   (b) $\dfrac{1}{2} - \dfrac{1}{4} = \dfrac{2}{4} - \dfrac{1}{4} = \dfrac{1}{4}$ kg

Page 43

1. $\dfrac{3}{8} + \dfrac{1}{4} = \dfrac{3}{8} + \dfrac{2}{8} = \dfrac{5}{8}$ litres

2. (a) $\dfrac{4}{5} + \dfrac{11}{15} = \dfrac{12}{15} + \dfrac{11}{15} = \dfrac{23}{15}$ km

(b) Jason ran further.

$$\frac{4}{5} - \frac{11}{15} = \frac{12}{15} - \frac{11}{15} = \frac{1}{15} \text{ km}$$

Page 44

1. Red   2. Yellow

3. (a) Yes

   (b) Orange and green

Page 45-46

1. 700 − 523 = 177

2. 300 − 156 = 144

3. (a) 248 + 176 = 424

   (b) 600 − 424 = 176

4. (a) 189 + 96 = 285

   (b) 400 − 285 = 115

5. (a) 398 + 275 = 673

   (b) 900 − 673 = 227

Page 47

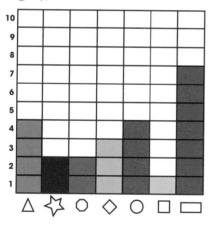

The rectangle

Page 48

Apple	5
Pear	4
Mango	2
Orange	1

Page 49

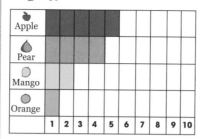

1. (a) Apple   (b) 5

2. (a) Orange   (b) 1

Page 50

Review that the treasures are drawn in the correct boxes on the treasure map.

Page 51

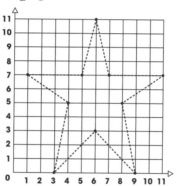

A star

Page 52–53

Answers will vary.

Page 54–55

1. 44, 8   2. 44, 40   3. 4, 40

4. 4, 8   5. 8, 12   6. 12, 16

7. 16, 20   8. 20, 24   9. 4, 36

10. 24, 20   11. 44, 36   12. 28, 24

13. 32, 20   14. 36, 16   15. 40, 12

16. 44, 8

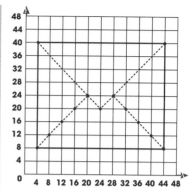

An envelope

Page 56–57

1. 4, 1   2. 9, 1   3. 9, 3   4. 2, 3

5. 8, 3   6. 8, 5   7. 8, 9   8. 6, 9

9. 6, 11   10. 7, 10   11. 6, 9   12. 4, 9

13. 4, 3

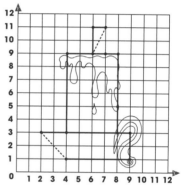

A candle

Page 58–59

1. 77, 49   2. 70, 63   3. 63, 77

4. 49, 70   5. 35, 63   6. 42, 14

7. 14, 7   8. 21, 7   9. 21, 21

10. 28, 21   11. 28, 14   12. 21, 14

13. 14, 14   14. 14, 7

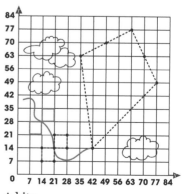

A kite

Page 60-61

1. 11, 8   2. 10, 9   3. 2, 9   4. 1, 8

5. 6, 1   6. 9, 8   7. 8, 9   8. 6, 1

9. 3, 8   10. 4, 9   11. 6, 9   12. 5, 8

13. 6, 1   14. 7, 8   15. 6, 9

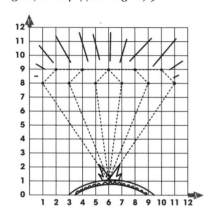

A diamond ring

Page 62-74

1. B   2. C   3. C   4. A

5. A   6. D   7. C   8. C

9. B   10. B   11. A   12. C

13. C   14. C   15. B   16. A

17. A   18. B   19. C   20. C

21. D   22. A   23. B   24. D

25. B   26. A   27. D   28. A

29. (a) Mother ate more.

$$\frac{1}{4} - \frac{1}{8} = \frac{2}{8} - \frac{1}{8} = \frac{1}{8}$$

(b) $\dfrac{1}{4} + \dfrac{1}{8} = \dfrac{2}{8} + \dfrac{1}{8} = \dfrac{3}{8}$

(c) $1 - \dfrac{3}{8} = \dfrac{8}{8} - \dfrac{3}{8} = \dfrac{5}{8}$

30. (a) $\dfrac{1}{2} + \dfrac{1}{4} = \dfrac{2}{4} + \dfrac{1}{4} = \dfrac{3}{4}$

(b) $\dfrac{3}{4} + \dfrac{1}{8} = \dfrac{6}{8} + \dfrac{1}{8} = \dfrac{7}{8}$

(c) $\dfrac{8}{8} - \dfrac{7}{8} = \dfrac{1}{8}$

31. B   32. D   33. D

34. Number of students

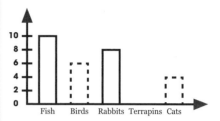

35. D   36. D   37. B   38. D

39.

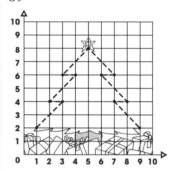

A Christmas tree

SCHOLASTIC
Learning Express

Congratulations!

I, _____

am a Scholastic Superstar!

Paste a photo or draw a
picture of yourself.

I have completed Fractions and Graphs L3.

Presented on _____